THE CHILDREN PRAY WITH ST BERNADETTE:

A children's prayer book

By Joseph Foroma

Copyright © 2025 Joseph Foroma.

THE CHILDREN PRAY WITH ST BERNADETTE:
A children's prayer

Paperback ISBN: 978-1-77934-479-3
E-Book ISBN: 978-1-77934-478-6

First Printed in 2025

All rights reserved. No part of this publication may be reproduced, distributed, or transmitted in any form or by any means, including photocopying, recording or other electronic or mechanical methods, without the prior written permission of the publishers. This book may not be lent, resold, hired out or otherwise disposed of by way of trade in any form, binding or cover other than that in which it is published, without the prior consent of the publishers.

Book design by Daniel Mutendi

Front and back cover designs by Daniel Mutendi

Photos:

The photos of Our Lady and those of St Bernadette were provided by and used with the kind permission of the Sanctuaire ND de Lourdes, Pôle Communication.

The children pray with St Bernadette

Introduction

"In the Name of the Father, and of the Son and of the Holy Spirit. Amen."

HAIL MARY

"Hail Mary, full of grace. The Lord is with thee. Blessed art thou among women, and blessed is the fruit of thy womb, Jesus.

"Holy Mary, Mother of God, pray for us sinners, now and at the hour of our death. Amen."

Glory be to God
Glory be to the Father,
to the Son and to the Holy Spirit.
As it was in the beginning,
Is now and ever shall be,
world without end. Amen.

This is a prayer book for you, little ones. You can read it alone or with your parents or guardians.

The story of Bernadette

Little Bernadette Soubirous was born in southern France in a little town called Lourdes. She was a prayerful young person. She always had her holy Rosary with her. She could pray the Rosary even as a very young girl. In 1858, between 11th February and 16th July (also the Feast of Our Lady of Mount Carmel), she encountered the Blessed Virgin Mary at the Grotto of Massabielle in Lourdes on 18 occasions in what are now called 18 Apparitions.

Sometimes, the lady spoke to Bernadette and at other times she did not speak. They would just quietly pray together at the grotto. She gave the young Bernadette very important messages about praying and going to Confession so that sins may be forgiven.

In this small booklet you will learn of some examples given us by Bernadette in each short prayer. You can use them to pray in the morning, at night or at any time of day. Or occasions such as First Holy Communion, Confirmation, birthday celebrations or Feast days.

This little booklet will help you along your journey to become a good child of our Lord Jesus Christ. Bernadette loved our Lord Jesus Christ and his Mother, the Blessed Virgin Mary. Do you wish to be a follower of Jesus Christ too, about whom Bernadette said, "He is all I need"?

Bernadette was the eldest child in a very poor family. She was baptized as a small baby, only two days old. As she grew up she always prayed the Rosary.

Bernadette was a sickly girl who experienced many difficulties in her life due to her poor health. But this did not take her away from her deep faith in God. She was kind and considerate, and played with other children, just as you do. But she was given the special grace of meeting the Blessed Virgin Mary.

She was given many messages by this "beautiful lady", now also known as Our Lady of Lourdes. The lady told her to pray for sinners and to ask people to pray and go for Confession so that their sins would be forgiven.

The lady told Bernadette to ask the priests to build a small chapel at Lourdes. She was to tell the priests to lead people in procession while saying their prayers. Some miracle cures happened at the grotto during Bernadette's encounters with the beautiful lady.

Eventually, at the 16th of the 18 Apparitions, the "beautiful lady" revealed to Bernadette who she really was. She told Bernadette, "**I am the Immaculate Conception**", meaning that she was Mary the Mother of Jesus Christ.

Little Bernadette is now a Saint in heaven. She loves you all, little children and wants to pray with you and for you. She wants you to grow up good children of Jesus Christ.

THE PRAYERS

PRAYER ONE: Bernadette and her family

Bernadette's family were very prayerful. Her mother and father loved each other very much. Bernadette herself played with her younger sister, Toinette. Later, she had some brothers and sisters whom she loved.

Let us pray

May I learn from the example of Bernadette to love my family and friends and all those who care for me. These people form for me the church at home which will lead me to heaven. There, I will meet Bernadette and all the Saints. How I wish that everyone I meet will be with me there too.

PRAYER TWO: Bernadette and faith

The lady told Bernadette, "*I cannot promise to make you happy in this world, but in the next*."

Bernadette was baptized when she was only 2 days old. That was her first introduction to the faith. Bernadette had very strong faith. On 11th February 1858, when she encountered the Blessed Virgin Mary for the first time, she had her Rosary on her. And at the age of 14 years she could already recite the Rosary. When she encountered this 1st Apparition, her first reaction was to pull out her rosary and begin to pray.

Let us pray
We pray that we always look up to the heavenly rewards of meeting with the Saints and rejoicing with them in the presence of our Lord Jesus Christ.

PRAYER THREE: Bernadette and obedience

Bernadette was always obedient to both her parents. She was obedient to the family in Batres whose sheep she looked after. Later, as a Nun in the Convent at Nevers, she obeyed her superiors even when asked to do difficult tasks when she was unwell.

Let us pray

Our Lord Jesus Christ, please teach me to obey my parents and guardians so that I may be like little Bernadette, who showed her love for you by obeying her parents and everyone responsible for her. When I go to sleep each night, may I find rest knowing I have been a good and obedient child.

PRAYER FOUR: The 18 Apparitions
"Go and drink at the spring and wash yourself there" (9th Apparition)

There were 18 Apparitions of the Blessed Lady, and on some occasions, the lady did not appear, but Bernadette still went back to the grotto – the lady had told her to "come back for 15 days" even though she did not appear on some of the days.

Bernadette was not embarrassed to do as the lady asked her. The lady told her to dig up mud and eat the grass at the Spring at the Grotto. She was not ashamed to do so in front of multitudes of people. The spring she dug up now provides water used by millions each year to drink and to pray. Many have received the graces of healing and hope by using it.

Let us pray

St Bernadette, I would like to go to Church every Sunday like you did and visit the grotto and other places of prayer. Teach us to have no shame to be children of the Lord Jesus Christ until we meet him in heaven.

PRAYER FIVE: Bernadette and praying the Holy Rosary

Little Bernadette learned to pray the Rosary at a young age from the example of her family. She was holding the holy Rosary when she first encountered the Virgin Mary at the grotto. She prayed the Rosary with "the beautiful lady".

Let us pray

St Bernadette, please teach me to pray everyday when I go to bed. Teach me to pray and thank the Lord when I wake up each morning. Teach me to pray before meals and to pray so that I may be a good child.

PRAYER SIX: Bernadette and sin

At the 8th Apparition, the lady said, "**Penance! Penance! Penance! Pray to God for sinners. Kiss the earth as a sign of penitence for sinners!**"

Bernadette hated sin. She was given as one of the key messages by the Virgin Mother to pray for sinners and that people would repent of their sins.

Let us pray

St Bernadette, please teach me to walk away from sin and to forgive others. When I sin, I offend the Sacred Heart of Jesus. Teach me to pray for other children across the whole world, especially those who are sick, who lack food and want to go to school.

PRAYER SEVEN: Bernadette and friends

On the day of the first Apparition, Bernadette was in the company of her sister and a friend, gathering firewood. We do not hear of bad friends in Bernadette's life.

Let us pray

Our Blessed Mother Mary, please help me to find good friends so that I may grow in your beauty. Teach me to follow only good things from those I meet and the friends I play with.

PRAYER EIGHT: Bernadette and the Blessed Mother ("the beautiful lady")

"*I looked at her as much as I could. She looked at me like a person talking to another person.*" Bernadette recounting the times she went to the grotto to meet the beautiful Lady whom she also called 'Arquero', underlining the deep, friendly relationship they shared.

Let us pray

St Bernadette, pray for me so that I may become like the beautiful Lady who taught you so much and whose example you shared with the world.

PRAYER NINE: Bernadette and humility
"*Who do you take me for? I know that if the Blessed Virgin chose me, it's because I was the most ignorant. If she had found one more ignorant than me, she would have chosen her.*" Bernadette responding to the residents of Lourdes as she stood her ground about the genuineness of her encounters with Our Lady. Her humility made her insist that she was not chosen for any other virtues other than her lowliness and poverty.

Let us pray

St Bernadette, teach me to be humble like you. So I would follow your example to be able to proudly stand by the Lord Jesus Christ, who died for me on the Cross.

PRAYER TEN: Caring for others

"*I like taking care of the poor. I like caring for the sick. I'll stay with the Sisters of Nevers.*" Bernadette shared the mercy and charity that has been carried by all of the Saints that we learn about. In the hospital, she looked after the sick and showed them great love.

Let us pray

How I too, wish to be like you so that those around me can see in me a good child who loves the Lord and cares for those in need. Lead and protect me so that I will continue to do this when I grow up.

PRAYER ELEVEN: Bernadette and serving others

"I'm the broom used by the Virgin. What do you do with a broom after you finish using it? You put it behind the door. That's my place. I'll stay there."

Let us pray

How so beautiful! St Bernadette, can you please teach us little children to be like you! Please teach us to be humble and know that the Lord is above all else. I pray for my friends too so that they are good and obedient children.

PRAYER TWELVE: Bernadette and quiet prayer

"*The grotto was my heaven*," Bernadette tells how much she loved to go to the grotto and spending time there. This is the grotto at St Gildard, Nevers and Bernadette said the statue there resembled the beautiful lady she used to meet at Massabielle in Lourdes more than all the other statues she had seen.

Let us pray

St Bernadette, teach me to create a place of prayer in my bedroom, in our house. And to go to Church every week and whenever that is possible. Teach me to find peace in the corner where I pray. And when the day comes to night, that my Guardian Angel will look after me as I sleep.

PRAYER THIRTEEN: Bernadette and putting others first

I will not forget anybody." Reflecting her profound love for others and how serving others was a natural attribute of hers.

Let us pray

Our Blessed Mother, teach me to remember everyone, especially those who are not as fortunate as me. Teach me to pray for the little children everywhere who have no one to care for them and those caught up in areas with wars and droughts.

PRAYER FOURTEEN: Bernadette and the will of God

"*I thought that God wanted it! When you think that God allowed it, you don't complain.*" Of her lifelong sufferings and illnesses, which she never complained about. Despite severe illnesses, pain and visible wounds around her knees, she continued to carry out her duties scrubbing Convent floors and other work assigned to her in the infirmary. This she did until it became physically impossible for her to carry on, without ever complaining.

Let us pray

Bernadette please teach me always to surrender everything to the Lord. For even when we are facing difficulties He always loves us and does the best for us. Whatever the Lord places in front of us, give me a heart to accept and never to complain.

PRAYER FIFTEEN: Bernadette and self-acceptance

"The Passion touches me more when I read it than when someone explains it to me."

Let us pray

Our Blessed Mother, you suffered together with your son, Our Lord Jesus Christ, as he was crucified for me on the Cross. Teach me to love you and to adore him because he suffered to give me life. Teach me to listen to your gentle words so that I may be a good child. St Bernadette, please teach me to accept myself as God has created me. And to love Him for what He has given me. Teach me to understand that illness and hardship cannot separate me from His great love for me.

PRAYER SIXTEEN: Bernadette and God only

"He is all I need"

We should not seek too many things in life but to be content with seeking God only. St Alphonsus encourages us, "*Let your constant practice be to offer yourself to God, that He may do with you what He pleases ... Since His delights are to be with you, let yours be to be found in Him.*"

"Jesus alone for Master". Bernadette made it clear her only master was the Lord Jesus Christ.

Let us pray

St Bernadette, I want to be like you. Please pray for me so that I may never depart from the Lord Jesus Christ and pray to Him every day of my life.

PRAYER SEVENTEEN: Bernadette and gratitude

"Help me to thank God to the very end"

A warning not to fail at the last hurdle. As highlighted in the book of Revelations about the glory of God. There are many who lead lives of righteousness only to then throw all the good work away at the very end.

Let us pray

Lord teach me to say thank you for each day when I wake up. Teach me to say thank you to my parents and guardians for all they do for me. Teach me to say thank you when someone is kind to me.

PRAYER EIGHTEEN: Bernadette and the Blessed Mother

Thursday 25th March 1858: The Immaculate Conception

The sixteenth apparition occurred on the Feast of the Annunciation on 25th March. The vision finally revealed her name to Bernadette. Bernadette recounted: "*She extended her arms towards the ground, then joined them as though in prayer and said **Que soy era Immaculada Concepciou** (I am the Immaculate Conception)*".

Let us pray

Our Lady and St Bernadette, please help me be a believer in the Word of God. Just like you believed and went back to the grotto as the beautiful lady had asked. Teach me to believe even when things are difficult for me to understand. My Blessed Mother, you were born without sin.

PRAYER NINETEEN: Bernadette and kindness
Bernadette looked after the sick in the Convent at Nevers. She was always kind to them and she loved her job. She did it even when she was unwell herself.

Let us pray
St Bernadette, teach me to be kind and compassionate to those who need help. Teach me to be patient with others when they ask for support. Teach me to show love when I do my work.

PRAYER TWENTY: Bernadette and spoken language

Bernadette was only a child herself. But she did not use bad words. She was able to correct others when they did not do the right thing.

Let us pray

St Bernadette, pray with me so that I never use bad words. That I may be seen by others as another little Bernadette.

PRAYER TWENTY-ONE: Bernadette and honesty

Bernadette refused to tell lies even when put under pressure by those in authority about what she had seen at the grotto. Some wanted her to change her account of what she had seen. She kept her word about what she had seen and heard from the "beautiful Lady".

Let us pray
St Bernadette help me to be like you, that I may tell no lies. That I may always stand for truth in front of others. Just as our Lord Jesus Christ wants us to do.

BACK PAGE

Joseph Foroma was born in Zimbabwe to devoutly Catholic parents. Following his earlier book, LOURDES: "*The Heart of God's Mercy – Accounts and Reflections of a Pilgrim.*" He has decided to write this short prayer book for use by children, parents and guardians. The story of Bernadette is one of hope, forgiveness, humility, perseverance, repentance and the boundless fountain spring of God's mercy.